CW00549606

it could have been yours

it could have been yours

The enlightened person's guide
to the year's most desirable things

Jolyon Fenwick and Marcus Husselby

PROFILE BOOKS

First published in Great Britain in 2011 by
PROFILE BOOKS LTD
3a Exmouth House
Pine Street
London EC1R 0JH
www.profilebooks.com

A CIP catalogue record for this book is available from the British Library.

ISBN 978 1 84668 490 6
eISBN 978 1 84765 757 2

Text design and layout by sue@lambledesign.demon.co.uk

Printed and bound in Britain by Butler Tanner and Dennis, Frome

Disclaimer
All reasonable efforts have been made by the authors to contact copyright
holders and to obtain all necessary copyright permissions for material
reproduced in this book. Copyright acknowledgements appear in the
Acknowledgements section on page 118, which for copyright purposes
is an extension of this page. Any omissions or errors of attribution are
unintentional and will, if brought to the attention of the authors and
publisher in writing, be corrected in future printings.

For D.F. and M.D.
W.E.H. and Dr J.L.H.

'Avarice, sphincter of the heart.'

Matthew Green (1696–1737), *The Spleen*

Foreword

We have been presumptuous enough to describe this book as an *enlightened* person's guide to the world's most desirable things – by which, I suppose, we simply mean that there may be more interesting things to buy than Cristal, superyachts and the other exalted paraphernalia of modern life.

As the subtitle suggests, most of the items contained within this book were sold or offered for sale during the period July 2010 to June 2011. The beadier-eyed among you will notice that there is the odd one that falls outside this time period, for which latitude we hope you will forgive us.

Jolyon Fenwick
Marcus Husselby
August 2011

Schindler's list

Manuscript, dated 18 April 1945, detailing the names, birth dates and occupations of 801 male Jewish workers employed in the enamelware and ammunitions factories of Oskar Schindler (1908–74). Typed on onion-skin paper, the 13-page document lists those individuals whom Schindler averred to the Nazis were essential to the war effort, thus saving them from the Holocaust. Belonging for 55 years to the family of Schindler's accountant, Itzhak Stern, the manuscript was offered for sale by Momentsintime.com in March 2010 for $2.2 million.

Marilyn Monroe's wonderbra

An early example of 'Hello Boys' lingerie engineering once belonging to Marilyn Monroe (1926–62). The bra, incorporating extra straps and four internal cups, appears to betray the secret of the star's winningly curvilinear bosom. Sold at auction by International Autograph Auctions in July 2010 for £3,200.

£3,200

$4,800

First photograph of a snowflake

One of ten snowflake photographs taken on 15 January 1885 by Vermont farmer and pioneer of photomicrography, Wilson A. Bentley (1865–1931). Aged only 19, self-educated Bentley caught the falling crystals on black velvet and, combining a bellows camera and a microscope, quickly photographed them before they melted. They are the first images of a snowflake ever recorded. In Bentley's words: 'Under the microscope, I found that snowflakes were miracles of beauty; and it seemed a shame that this beauty should not be seen and appreciated by others. Every crystal was a masterpiece of design, and no one design was ever repeated. When a snowflake melted, that design was lost for ever.' Bentley died of pneumonia on 23 December 1931, after walking six miles home in a blizzard. Offered for sale at the American Antiques Show in New York in January 2010 for $4,800.

The Trafalgar Jack

7ft 4in x 11ft 7in Union Jack flag flown from HMS *Spartiate* during the Battle of Trafalgar, 21 October 1805. Following the battle, the flag, bearing the shot and shell splinter scars of the conflict, was presented by the 640-strong crew to Fife-born Lieutenant James Clephan, one of the highest honours to be bestowed on an officer by his men. Owned for 204 years by Clephan's descendants, the only surviving Union Jack from Nelson's momentous victory was sold at auction by Charles Miller in October 2009 for £384,000, 20 times its estimated price.

£384,000

Berlusconi's bed

??????

Four-poster bed, complete with canopy, bronze fittings and eagle heads, once belonging to Napoleon Bonaparte (1769–1821).
A silent witness to the age-old human link between power, libido and diminutive size, the bed was bought by Silvio Berlusconi (1936–) in February 2010. Ever the pragmatist, Berlusconi immediately requested that the bed be widened. Sold by Rome antiques dealer Anna Quattrini for an undisclosed sum.

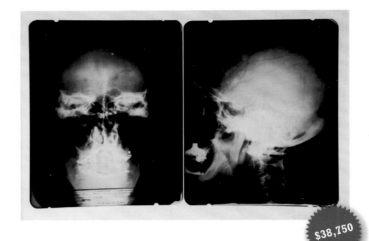

$38,750

Einstein's brain

X-ray scan, taken in 1945, showing the brain of Albert Einstein (1879–1955). The correlation between neuroanatomy and general or mathematical intelligence has long been debated. Weighing in at 1,230 grams, Einstein's brain (removed after his death and now cut into 240 1cm³ pieces) was actually smaller than that of the average modern human. A 1999 anatomical study, however, did reveal that the great physicist's grey matter contained a number of unusual anomalies – most importantly that his parietal lobes, the area of the brain usually connected to spatial and visual recognition, were 15 per cent wider than average. The exact significance of this irregularity is clearly difficult to establish, owing to the infrequent availability of geniuses' brains to examine. The X-ray was sold by Julien's Auctions in December 2010 for $38,750, 20 times the original estimate.

Walkabout Creek

The Walkabout Creek Hotel, located in the small town of McKinlay, Queensland, made famous as the favourite outback watering-hole of Mick 'Crocodile' Dundee in Peter Faiman's 1986 film.
Offered for sale in October 2010 for A$1.25 million.

A$1.25m

The Land of Hope and Glory

Catrigg Force. Over six acres of lush wooded valley with waterfall, a mile from Stainforth in North Yorkshire. The commercially valueless piece of land is believed to have been the inspiration for Sir Edward Elgar's 1902 'Pomp and Circumstance March No. 1', on the 'trio' theme to which, after the suggestion of King Edward VII, A. C. Benson's famous 'Land of Hope and Glory' lyrics were set. In a 2006 BBC survey, 55 per cent of those polled wanted 'Land of Hope and Glory' to replace 'God Save the Queen' as the British national anthem. The pocket of land was offered for sale in January 2010 for £25,000.

£25,000

£14,600

'God Save the Queen'

10in acetate, used as a test pressing for the Sex Pistols' hit 'God Save
the Queen'. Released on 27 May 1977 as the band's second single
and featuring on their only album, *Never Mind the Bollocks, Here's
the Sex Pistols*, the song caused much controversy, due chiefly to its
equation of Her Majesty with the 'fascist regime' and its recurring
claim that the country had 'no future'. It reached number one on
the NME charts in the United Kingdom, but only made it to number
two on the official UK Singles Chart as used by the BBC, amidst
accusations that the chart had been 'fixed'. Cut at The Town House
Studios in London, having been recorded at London's Wessex
Studios in March 1977, this rare test pressing was sold on eBay in
April 2011 for £14,600.

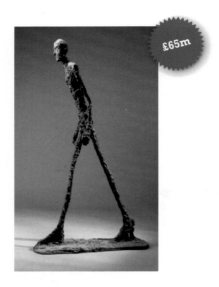

Walking Man I

L'Homme qui marche I (*Walking Man I*) by Alberto Giacometti (1901–66). The most expensive work of art in history, the bronze sculpture was sold at auction by Sotheby's in February 2010 for £65,001,250.

Lehman Brothers mug

Lehman Brothers mug bearing the legend 'Where vision gets built'. On 15 September 2008, the firm filed for Chapter 11 bankruptcy protection following the massive exodus of most of its clients, drastic losses in its stock and devaluation of its assets by credit-rating agencies. The filing marked the largest bankruptcy in US history. Sold on eBay in May 2010 for $45.

$45

£600

The last tot

Since 1655, when Jamaica was captured from Spain, seamen of the British Royal Navy had become happily accustomed to receiving their regulation daily ration* of rum on board His or Her Majesty's ships. Following a debate in the House of Commons, however, which concluded that the consumption of rum was incompatible with the sound operation of modern weapons and navigational technology, the cherished tradition was terminated, and on 31 July 1970 (known as 'Black Tot Day'), the pipe of 'Up spirits' was heard in the Royal Navy for the last time. The day was widely marked as one of mourning by sailors. Black armbands were worn as the Queen was toasted. Tots of rum were buried at sea and in one navy training camp sailors paraded a black coffin flanked by drummers and a piper. This bottle of Black Tot rum, one of 6,000 bottles containing the final remnants of the Royal Navy's 1970 regulation supply, was offered for sale – together with a copper cup for measuring the official half-gill ration – on HMS *Belfast* on 31 July 2010 for £600.

*Up until 1740, the regulation daily ration for sailors of the Royal Navy was an eye-watering half a pint of neat rum, issued twice a day. Ever suspicious that they were not receiving their dues, sailors would verify their rum had not been diluted by pouring it on to gunpowder and setting light to it, hence the term 'proof'. By volume, 57.15 per cent alcohol has been calculated as the minimum required for it to pass the test. By 1970, the daily rum ration, doled out by the rum bo'sun at midday, had unsurprisingly been reduced to a more temperate eighth of a pint (neat for senior ratings, watered down for juniors).

Casanova's memoirs

Histoire de ma vie. The memoirs and autobiography of Giacomo
Girolamo Casanova de Seingalt (1725–98), the Venetian poet,
adventurer and Lothario. The yellowing 3,500-page manuscript,
censored until 1960, details the conquest of over 100 women,
possibly some men and one nun. Bought by an anonymous
donor on behalf of the Bibliothèque Nationale de
France in February 2011 for £4.4 million. The most
expensive manuscript in history.

£4.4m

Wall Street

Cobalt-blue porcelain 'Wall Street' sign, framed in wrought iron and dating from between 1890 and 1920. Stood on the corner of New York's Wall Street and Broad Street. Offered for sale by Christie's in June 2010 for $116,500.

DOWNING STREET

Downing Street

Cast-iron 'Downing Street' sign that hung on the corner of London's Downing Street and Whitehall in the 1890s. Offered for sale by Bonhams in January 2010 with an estimate of £6,000–£8,000.

£6,000–£8,000

'Harry'

Second World War prisoner-of-war diary of one Private
William MacDonald, containing pencil and watercolour
sketches of the famous Allied escape tunnel from Stalag Luft III.
The escape operation, brought to wider public consciousness by the
1963 film *The Great Escape*, involved the excavation by over 600 Allied
airmen of three separate tunnels, codenamed by the prisoners as
'Tom', 'Dick' and 'Harry'. Three were dug, on the assumption that
if German guards discovered one, they would never dream that any
others were being attempted. In March 1944, 76 men crawled the
348 feet to freedom through 'Harry' – the single greatest escape of
the war. Unfortunately 73 of the escapees were soon recaptured, of
whom 50 were later shot by the Nazis in one of the more notorious
episodes of the war. The diary was sold at auction by Lyon and
Turnbull in February 2010 for £4,000.

Bond's DB5

1964 Aston Martin DB5 featuring in the 007 films *Goldfinger* (1964) and *Thunderball* (1965). Connery's motor, complete with revolving licence plates, ejector seat and bulletproof shield, and still capable of 145 mph and 0–60 mph in 7.1 seconds, was bought in October 2010 at a London auction for £2.6 million by American collector Harry Yeaggy, who will display the car at a museum in Ohio. It is worth noting that Ian Fleming's literary creation never drove such a car, favouring a grey 1933 4.5-litre Bentley convertible with the Amherst Villiers supercharger.

£2.6m

Houdini's handcuffs

1905 nickel-plated Bean-Cobb handcuffs once
belonging to Hungarian-born American magician
and escapologist Harry Houdini (1874–1926). After
many unsuccessful years as a playing-card magician,
it was through his seemingly unaccountable ability to escape from
handcuffs that Houdini rose to fame, most notably in 1900, when
he demonstrated his powers at Scotland Yard in front of a number
of bemused police constables. It has never been clear quite how the
'Handcuff King' performed his frequently death-defying feats of
freedom, but a widely speculated theory points to an almost unique
ability to regurgitate keys and other tools at will. Harry Houdini
died of peritonitis, secondary to a ruptured appendix reportedly
caused by a McGill University student, J. Gordon Whitehead, who
delivered multiple blows to Houdini's abdomen to test Houdini's
claim that he was able to take any blow to the body above the waist
without injury. The handcuffs were offered for sale by Potter and
Potter Auctions of Chicago in May 2011 with an estimate of $3,500.

$3,500

Playboy bunny

£5,950

Original Playboy bunny costume as worn in Hugh Hefner's 1960s London Playboy Club at 45 Park Lane. Sporting the lepidoral uniform of a Playboy bunny girl was a much coveted ambition for many an aspiring showbiz girl of the time. Both Lauren Hutton and Debbie Harry were at one time bunnies. But the selection process was rigorous. As well as being required to identify 143 brands of liquor and to garnish 20 different cocktail variations, bunny girls – including the Door Bunny, Cigarette Bunny, Floor Bunny, Playmate Bunny and Jet Bunny (a waitress who served on the Playboy Jet) – had to master the three trademark bunny manoeuvres: the Bunny Stance (legs together, back arched and hips tucked under), the Bunny Perch (sitting straight-backed on the back of a chair, sofa, or railing within beckoning distance of a patron) and the famous Bunny Dip (a graceful lean backwards while bending at the knees with the left knee lifted and tucked behind the right leg, allowing the bunnies to serve drinks while keeping their low-cut costume in place). The bunnies were kept an eye on by 'undercover patrons', with the opportunity to 'date' the girls being limited to the most important C1 'Keyholder' members of the club. Not everyone was impressed, however, with Clive James once drily opining that, 'to make it as a bunny, a girl needed more than just looks. She needed idiocy, too.' Once apparently belonging to 'Erica', this original bunny costume (a replica of which forms part of the collection of the Smithsonian Museum) was offered for sale by Paul Fraser Collectibles in April 2011 for £5,950.

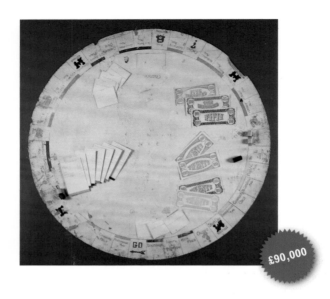

£90,000

Original Monopoly

1933 set of Monopoly, featuring the place names and railways from Atlantic City, New Jersey, hand-painted by Charles B. Darrow, the man most commonly recognised as the inventor of the famous board game. After witnessing his neighbours' enthusiasm for playing a game whose object was to buy and sell property, Darrow, an unemployed domestic-heater salesman from Germantown, Philadelphia, decided to devise a version of his own. After several failed attempts to sell the rights to the game, Darrow successfully secured US Patent 2,026,082 on Monopoly, which was acquired by Parker Brothers in 1936. Within a year, 20,000 sets of the game were being produced every week – the royalties from which made Darrow the first board-game-inventor millionaire. This 'original' Monopoly set was sold at auction by Sotheby's in February 2011 for £90,000.

Banksy's real name

Much journalistic speculation has inevitably surrounded the true identity of the anonymous graffiti artist known as 'Banksy'. The only solid autobiographical fact known about him appears to be that he was born and raised in Bristol. It has been widely rumoured that he is in fact called John Banks (birthday 28 July 1973), and that his parents still think he is a successful painter and decorator. In 2008, the *Mail on Sunday* claimed to have unmasked the artist as suburban former public schoolboy Robin Gunningham, a claim routinely refuted by Banksy's agent. In the latest episode, an American Internet seller, going by the alias of 'jaybuysthings', offered to supply a piece of paper bearing Banksy's real name to the highest bidder on eBay, confidently asserting that he had solved the mystery by matching up sales and dates with tax returns. The January 2011 auction was pulled after only a few days with the highest bid standing at $999,999. It is unclear whether the identity was revealed or if the money changed hands, or indeed if the seller was Banksy himself.

$999,999

Ahmadinejad's Peugeot

$2.5m

1977 Peugeot 504 belonging to the sixth president of
the Islamic Republic of Iran, Mahmoud Ahmadinejad
(1956–). The car, which Mr Ahmadinejad made his trademark mode
of transport during his tenure as mayor of Tehran (though he was
rarely seen inside it after becoming president in 2005), was put up
for auction in January 2011 in an effort to help fulfil a campaign
promise to put a roof over the head of every Iranian. The semi-
official Iranian news agency later claimed that the car (with a local
value in the region of $1,200) had been sold to a fellow Arab for the
sum of $2.5 million.

Maggie's handbag

Black Asprey handbag owned by Margaret Hilda Thatcher,
Baroness Thatcher (1925–), during her time as prime minister.
A much-flaunted symbol of her primacy in cabinet ('the handbag
is here', Nicholas Ridley was heard to say at the beginning of one
meeting), this particular accessory witnessed some of the Iron
Lady's most important summit meetings with Ronald Reagan and
Mikhail Gorbachev in the early 1980s. Donated by the
Baroness, the bag was offered for sale by Christie's in
June 2011 with an estimate of £100,000.

£100,000

Sullenberger's A320 Airbus

A320 Airbus aircraft piloted to safety by Captain Chesley 'Sully' Sullenberger, an act of deliverance that came to be known as the 'Miracle on the Hudson'. On 15 January 2009, US Airways Flight 1549 took off from Runway 4, LaGuardia airport, at 3.24:56 p.m., bound for Charlotte, North Carolina, with 150 passengers and five crew on board. Three minutes into the flight, the aircraft collided with a flock of Canada geese. The windscreen quickly turned dark brown and several loud thuds were heard. Both engines ingested the birds and immediately lost almost all thrust. Taking over the controls from first officer Jeffrey B. Skiles, Captain Sullenberger vainly explored the possibilities for an emergency landing but quickly concluded: 'We can't do it. We're gonna be in the Hudson.' While heading south at about 130 knots (150 mph) and giving a 'Brace for impact' call to the passengers, Sullenberger performed an unpowered ditch of the plane in the middle of the North River section of the Hudson River, roughly abeam 50th Street in Manhattan. Despite five serious injuries, all 155 souls were evacuated alive from the stricken craft. Speaking with news anchor Katie Couric, Sullenberger said, 'One way of looking at this might be that for 42 years, I've been making small, regular deposits in this bank of experience, education and training. And on January 15 the balance was sufficient so that I could make a very large withdrawal.' The Guild of Air Pilots and Air Navigators

FREE

awarded the entire flight crew of Flight 1549 a Master's Medal on
22 January 2009. A few weeks after the crash, it was revealed that
Sullenberger had lost a library book in the plane's cargo hold.
When Sullenberger telephoned the library to notify them of the
lost book, it waived the usual fees. Sullenberger's aircraft, minus
its two engines and described as having severe water damage
throughout the airframe and impact damage to its underside, was
offered at auction in February 2011, but was later donated to the
Carolinas Aviation Museum in Charlotte, North Carolina, by Chartis
Insurance, the aircraft's insurer. Price: Free.

Stirling's Purdeys

A pair of 12-bore self-opening sidelock ejector shotguns by James Purdey & Sons once owned by Colonel William Stirling (1912–83), one of the two brothers who founded the Special Air Service. Together with Robert Blair 'Paddy' Mayne (1915–55), Stirling formed 2 SAS in 1943, after his younger brother David, the original founder of 'The Regiment', was captured by the Germans. The guns were sold at auction by Bonhams in December 2010 for £42,000, twice the original estimate.

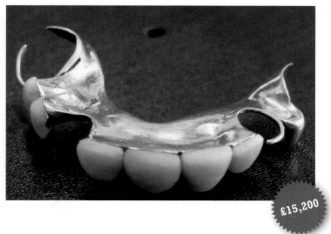

£15,200

Churchill's false teeth

Set of dentures once belonging to wartime prime minister
Winston S. Churchill (1874–1965). Created by dental technician
Derek Cudlipp, the dentures were specially designed to preserve
Churchill's famous lisp. So vital to the war effort was Cudlipp's
work deemed that the premier reportedly tore up the dentist's
enlistment papers in front of him. Sold at auction by Keys
Auctioneers in Aylsham, Norfolk, in July 2010 for £15,200.

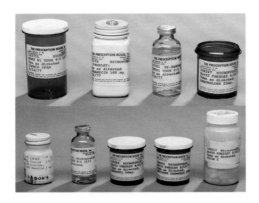

Elvis's medicine cabinet

Nine pill bottles issued by Dr George Nichopoulos
to Elvis Presley the day before his death on 16 August
1977. For more than a decade Elvis had indulged a titanic
appetite for prescription drugs – first to treat a chronic
sleep disorder and then to sustain 'the King' through the punitive
work schedule imposed by his manager, 'Colonel' Tom Parker
(an average of one show every other day from 1969 until June 1977,
and a three-album-a-year schedule for RCA). Presley's use and
knowledge of uppers, downers, laxatives, narcotics, hormones and
shots was encyclopedic, and a copy of *The Physician's Desk Reference*, a
comprehensive guide to legal drugs and their uses, never failed to
accompany him on tour. On top of the 14 drugs found in his system
at his autopsy, Elvis was known to have tried dilaudid, percodan,
placidyl, dexedrine (a rare 'upper', prescribed at the time as a 'diet
pill'), biphetamine, tiunal, desbutal, escatrol, amytal, quaaludes,
carbrital, seconal, methadone and ritalin. The cause of Elvis's death
was officially recorded as 'fatal heart arrhythmia' – a heart attack
– but in 1980, Dr Nichopoulos, his personal physician from 1970
to 1977 and pall-bearer at his funeral, was indicted on 14 counts

$46,327

of over-prescribing drugs to Presley and Jerry Lee Lewis, as well as 12 other patients. The district attorney ruled out murder charges because of the conflicting medical opinions about the cause of Presley's death. In 1977 alone, Nichopoulos had prescribed over 10,000 doses of amphetamines, barbiturates, narcotics, tranquillisers, sleeping pills, laxatives and hormones for Presley. He was charged with over-prescribing controlled substances to Presley during the final months before his death, but was acquitted by the Tennessee Board of Medical Examiners. At the age of 81, Nichopoulos decided to auction the bottles, considering himself too old to continue his touring show of Elvis's personal and intimate objects around the local casinos of America. They were sold as separate lots by Julien's Auctions in June 2009 for a total of $46,327.

HMS *Invincible*

17,000-ton aircraft carrier, built at Barrow-in-Furness by Vickers Ship Building and Engineering, serving in the Royal Navy from 1973 to 2005 before being decommissioned. Destined for a future as saucepans and razor blades, the great Falklands War carrier, offered for sale on the Disposal Service Authority website in March 2011, was bought by Turkish ship recyclers for £2 million.

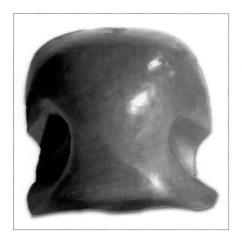

The Statue of Liberty's nose

$150,000+

A 2ft-wide piece of copper sheeting, being the tip and area around the nostrils of the Statue of Liberty's nose.* The nose was constructed in 1983 by Joseph Fieberger, a Manhattan-based metal artisan commissioned to renovate Frédéric Bartholdi's 1886 statue in time for its centennial. Five noses were constructed in total, and the impressions were made to an accuracy of six 10,000ths of an inch per foot. Of the remaining four, one was used for destructive testing, one was used for fastening plates, one is in a private collection and one, of course, can be found 140 feet above Liberty Island. Erosion of the statue is perhaps not so surprising when one finds out that the tip of the Lady's nose had been hammered to the thickness of a strand of human hair. Offered for sale by Guernsey's, New York, in September 2010, with an estimate of $150,000–$200,000.

*The full length of the nose on the statue is 4ft 6in. For those that are interested, Lady Liberty's waistline comes in at 35ft.

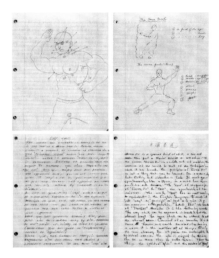

Bruce Lee's instruction manual

8.5in x 11in spiral-bound notebook belonging to martial arts legend Bruce Lee (1940–73). Containing over 35 pages of hand-drawn illustrations and Lee's handwritten reflections on the philosophy of his art, the material was intended to be published in a book entitled *The Tao of Chinese Gung Fu*. The project appears to have been thwarted by Lee's tragically premature death from cerebral oedema on 10 May 1973. As Lee wrote: 'Gung Fu is a special kind of skill; a fine art rather than just a physical exercise or self-defense. The principles of Gung Fu cannot be learned, like a science, by fact finding and instruction in facts. It must give spontaneously, like a flower, in a mind free from emotions and desires.' The notebook was sold through Paul Fraser Collectibles in May 2010 for £100,000.

£100,000

Chaplin's cane

$7,320

Bamboo cane once belonging to Sir Charles Spencer Chaplin (1889–1977). On 9 May 1953, the young son of the owner of an antiques shop in Lausanne, of which Chaplin was a regular patron, proudly showed the great comic actor a picture he had drawn. Chaplin signed the picture with the words 'very good' and gave the boy his cane. The cane, together with the picture, was sold by Bonhams in June 2010 for $7,320.

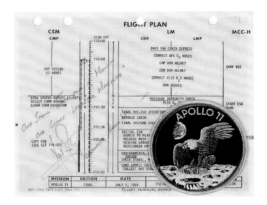

Armstrong's lines

Flight plan from the first moon landing, signed by Neil Alden Armstrong (1930–). The document (inscribed in quarantine by Armstrong on his return to earth and handed to NASA press officer John McLeaish) bears the words: 'ONE SMALL STEP FOR A MAN – ONE GIANT LEAP FOR MANKIND'. The document suggests that Armstrong, by omitting the indefinite article when he spoke his famous words at 2.56 UTC 21 July 1969 to half a billion people, had in fact fluffed his lines and lost the sense of the phrase. Understandably, and one has to feel quite rightly, Armstrong later expressed his preference that written quotations include the 'a' in parentheses. Sold by Bonhams in July 2010 for $152,000.

$152,000

'The Star Spangled Banner'

$506,500

First edition of the 1814 music and lyrics of 'The Star Spangled Banner'. The lyrics of the song come from 'Defence of Fort McHenry', a poem written by the 35-year-old lawyer and amateur poet Francis Scott Key (1779–1843) after witnessing the bombardment of Fort McHenry in Chesapeake Bay by British Royal Navy ships in 1812. 'The Star Spangled Banner' was made the national anthem of the USA by a congressional resolution on 3 March 1931. The last surviving copy of only 11 in existence, the document was sold by Christie's in Manhattan in December 2010 for $506,500.

Mike D's VW medallion

VW medallion (3^1/$_2$in) and chain (21in) worn by Beastie Boys'
vocalist Michael Diamond (1965–) in the mid-1980s. The
international trend inspired by Diamond's choice of neckwear
precipitated such a rash of vehicular vandalism that Volkswagen,
panicked by the prospect of a collapse in sales, ran an ad campaign
with coupons you could fill in to get your own VW badge. Belonging
to the collection of photographer Ricky Powell, the medallion
was sold at auction by Freeman's in September 2010
for $1,500.

$1,500

$25,000

Al Pacino's 'little friend'

'Say hello to my little friend.' M-16A1 machine gun wielded by Al Pacino's doomed and cocaine-fuelled character Tony Montana in the final scene of Brian De Palma's *Scarface* (1983). Pacino, a renowned method actor, insisted that his weapon was the correct weight, so he used a real, live-firing, fully automatic machine gun with grenade launcher. Also wielded by Arnold Schwarzenegger four years later in the 1987 film *Predator*, the (by then safe) M-16A1 was offered for sale by RM Auctions, Indiana, in 2010, with the highest bid being $25,000.

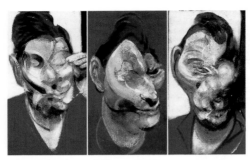

Bacon's Freud

Three Studies for a Portrait of Lucian Freud, 1965, triptych oil painting by Francis Bacon (1909–92) of his friend Lucian Freud (1922–2011). Sold at auction by Sotheby's in February 2011 for £23,001,250, three times its estimate.

£23m

Freud's Freud

£2.8m

Self-Portrait with a Black Eye, 1978, oil painting by
Lucian Freud (1922–2011). Freud had sustained the injury in a fight
with a taxi driver. Sold at auction by Sotheby's in February 2010 for
£2,841,250.

Kate Middleton's dress

Silk see-through dress modelled by Miss Catherine Middleton
during a 2002 fashion show at St Andrews University – the moment,
it is popularly speculated, at which Prince William fell for his future
bride. Belonging to its designer, Charlotte Todd, the
dress was sold at the Passion for Fashion auction in
March 2011 for £78,000.

£78,000

£1,250

Nazi £20 note

Counterfeit £20 note, backdated October 1937, manufactured during the Second World War by Jewish prisoners for the Nazis' Operation Bernhard. Directed by SS Major Bernhard Krüger (after whom it was codenamed), the operation, documented in the Oscar-winning 2007 Austrian film *The Counterfeiters*, was a plan devised by the SS to destabilise the British economy by flooding the country with forged Bank of England £5, £10, £20 and £50 notes. Between 1942 and April 1945, 142 counterfeiters, drawn chiefly from the Sachsenhausen concentration camp, produced 8,965,080 banknotes with a total value of £134,610,810. The notes are considered among the most perfect forgeries ever produced. British intelligence, however, got wind of the scheme in 1939 and countered the plot so successfully (by stopping printing any notes with a greater denomination than £5) that the Bank of England recorded just one as having been paid out. Notes with denominations greater than £5 were not reintroduced until the early 1960s (£10), 1970 (£20) and 1980 (£50). The note was sold by Mullock's auction house in Ludlow, Shropshire, in September 2010 for £1,250.

Custer's last flag

$2.2m

27ft 6in x 33ft silk guidon recovered from the field of
the Battle of the Little Bighorn. The most notorious
action in the American Indian wars, which came to be known as
'Custer's last stand', the battle saw 700 officers and men of the
US Seventh Cavalry under the command of Lieutenant Colonel
George Armstrong Custer (1839–76) face around 3,500 Lakota,
Northern Cheyenne and Arapaho Indians near the Little Bighorn
River in eastern Montana on 25 June 1876. Ineptly led by Custer and
numerically overwhelmed, the white men were squarely defeated,
268 cavalrymen being killed, including Custer himself. The 34-star
flag was found, bloodstained and bullet-holed, by a burial party
three days after the battle, pinned beneath the body of Corporal
John Foley, one of the only soldiers left unmutilated and capable of
being identified. The flag was sold at auction by Sotheby's in New
York in December 2010 for $2.2 million.

Fibonacci's *Book of Calculation*

Liber Abaci. 15th-century text of historic manuscript on arithmetic by
Leonardo Pisano Bigollo (c. 1170–c. 1250), nicknamed 'Fibonacci'.
Widely credited with bringing the Hindu-Arabic numeral system to
Europe, Fibonacci's *Book of Calculation* persuasively presented the
utility and benefits of the now familiar style of numerals (1, 2, 3, 4,
5, 6, 7, 8 and 9, of course) and the symbol for zero by applying them
to the practical world of book-keeping, weights and measures,
and trade. Swapping the abacus for the essential elements of the
decimal system, Fibonacci's text formed the basis for the modern
mathematical equations and sequences used today in computer
programming and the financial markets, thus shaping the history
of the western world. One of only 12 copies dating from the 13th
to the 15th century in existence, the manuscript was
offered for sale by Bonhams in New York in June 2011
with an estimate of $120,000–$180,000.

$120,000+

Blackadder's codpiece

Leather codpiece worn by Rowan Atkinson as the character Edmund Blackadder in the 1986 BBC series *Blackadder II*. The codpiece (from the Middle English 'cod', meaning scrotum) began life in the 14th century as a triangular piece of fabric covering the gap between gentlemen's separate-legged hose. As time passed, the appendages became shaped and padded to emphasise rather than to conceal, reaching their peak of flamboyance around 1540 before falling out of vogue in the 1590s. Sold by Cameo Auctioneers in Midgham, Berkshire, for £850.

£850

$1.5m $1.075m $1.1m

The birth of Superman, Batman and Spiderman

Comic books featuring the debut appearances of Superman (June 1938), Batman (May 1939) and Spiderman (February 1962). The comparative supremacy of the three superheroes has been the subject of playground speculation for the last five decades. On the evidence of the spate of recent auctions, it would seem that – commercially at least – Jerry Siegel and Joe Shuster's Kryptonite humanoid narrowly outdoes his chiropteric and arachnid rivals. The comics were sold at auction in March 2011 for $1.5 million, $1.075 million and $1.1 million respectively.

Galileo's fingers

Middle finger and thumb removed from the body of 'the father of modern science', Galileo Galilei (1564–1642). Condemned by the Catholic Church in 1632 for his doggedly heliocentric beliefs, Galileo spent the last ten years of his life under house arrest. As a heretic, he was buried on unconsecrated ground. In 1737, however, as the Copernican world view gained sway, Galileo's body was exhumed and transferred for Christian burial to the main body of the Basilica of Santa Croce in Florence. Prior to the committal, the thumb and two fingers, along with a tooth and a vertebra, were cut from Galileo's corpse by the laymen and masons that attended the ceremony. Up until 1905, these 'secular relics' were on display in a museum before the thumb and finger went missing. They reappeared at an auction in 2010 where they were anonymously purchased for an undisclosed sum. The digits are now on display in the History of Science Museum in Florence. It is not clear if the middle one is pointed at the Vatican.

??????

£133,250

Apple-1

1976 Apple-1 Personal Computer No. 82. The Apple-1s, personally despatched from Steve Jobs's parents' garage, were the first computers to 'work straight out of the box'. This particular machine came with its manuals showing the company's original logo of Newton sitting underneath an apple tree. It comprised just 8k of RAM. The latest iMac offers 16G, more than two million times more. Originally priced at a beastly $666.66, Computer No. 82 was sold at auction by Christie's in November 2010 for £133,250, just shy of its £150,000 estimate.

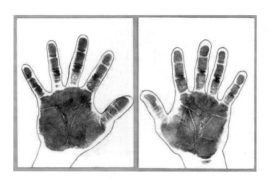

The Duke's hands

Ink prints, dated 16 February 1943, made with the hands of 'Duke' Paoa Kahinu Mokoe Hulikohola Kahanamoku (1890–1968), the Hawaiian father of surfing. A five-times Olympic medallist in swimming, Kahanamoku's proficiency in the water was attributed to his vast hands (9in long and nearly 6in wide). In 1929, the 'Duke' surfed a wave for over a mile at Waikiki Beach, still the longest ride recorded to date. The 'Duke's hands' were offered for sale at auction by Bonhams & Butterfields in October 2009, with an estimate of $8,000–$12,000.

$8,000–$12,000

£3.8m

Samson

66-million-year-old Tyrannosaurus rex skeleton. Measuring 15 feet high and 40 feet long, the female (strangely named 'Samson') comprises 170 bones and is the largest 'Tyrant Lizard King' ever discovered. Offered for sale at auction by Bonhams & Butterfields in October 2009, with an estimate of £3.8 million.

Stock Exchange clocks

£2,900–£9,400

Original nine London Stock Exchange clocks installed at
Threadneedle Street in 1971. Made by Italian manufacturers
Solari & Co., the electronic clocks measure 89 x 61 x 20cm and bear
the names of nine cities. Sold at auction at No. 1 Lombard Street in
September 2010, the following prices were realised: San Francisco
£5,000; New York £8,000; Toronto £3,000; London £9,400;
Johannesburg £2,900; Zurich £3,500; Tokyo £5,000; Melbourne
£3,500. Hong Kong failed to sell.

£50,000

Nelson's Column

4ft 6in Bath stone model of Nelson's Column. Created by the architect and original designer of the column, William Railton (c. 1801–77), the carved model confirms that the memorial to Nelson's great 1805 victory now standing in Trafalgar Square is in fact 30 feet shorter than Railton intended. The height of the column, built in Dartmoor granite between 1840 and 1843 (at a cost of £47,000), was reduced to its existing 169 feet due to lack of funds. So piqued was Railton by the reduction that he refused to attended the unveiling of the monument. Offered for sale by Bonhams in November 2010, with an estimate of £50,000.

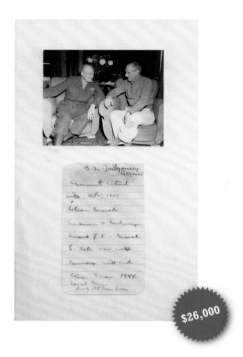

$26,000

Ike's bet

Lined slip of paper, signed by Field Marshal Bernard Law
Montgomery (1887–1976) and General Dwight David Eisenhower
(1890–1969), outlining the terms of a wager between the two men.
The note, a symbolic memento of the somewhat testy relationship
between the two Allied commanders, was written at the time by an
aide-de-camp, Colonel Ernest Lee, and reads: 'Agreement entered
into, Oct 11, 1943, between Generals Eisenhower & Montgomery
Amount £5—General E bets war with Germany will end before
Xmas 1944. Local Time'. The bet (lost of course by 'Ike', by a little
over four months) was sold by Alexander Auctions, Connecticut, in
February 2010 for $26,000.

Darth Vader

Complete Darth Vader costume made for use in George Lucas's
1980 film *The Empire Strikes Back*. Designed by Bermans & Nathans
and John Mollo, the costume of the character (voiced by James Earl
Jones, but physically inhabited in the film by bodybuilder Dave
Prowse) is said to have been based around five essential elements: a
monk's cloak, a Second World War German helmet, a gas mask, a
motorcycle undersuit and a medieval breastplate. The fallen
Jedi Knight's outfit was offered for sale at auction
by Christie's in November 2010, with an estimate of
£160,000–£230,000.

£160,000+

Concorde's speedo

Machmeter from Concorde G-Boad (210). The 7in-long instrument
recorded the speed of the aircraft during its record-breaking flight
in 1996 from New York to London lasting 2 hours, 52 minutes and
59 seconds. The dial displays the numbers 202, denoting twice the
speed of sound. Presented in 2003 to engineer Peter Gravestock in
acknowledgement of his long service with British Airways, the
machmeter was sold at auction on behalf of the family
by Lawrences of Crewkerne, Somerset, in March 2011
for £4,500.

£4,500

Max Yasgur's farm sign

??????

Original two-sided metal sign from Max Yasgur's
Dairy Farm near the hamlet of White Lake in the town
of Bethel, New York, site of the Woodstock Music & Art Fair. Billed
as 'An Aquarian Exposition: 3 Days of Peace & Music', Woodstock
played host to 32 acts and 500,000 love-filled fans from 15 to 18
August 1969. One of the pivotal moments in popular music history,
the festival was listed among *Rolling Stone*'s 50 Moments That
Changed the History of Rock and Roll. The day after the festival, a
White Lake local, noticing the sign had been knocked off its post
and was lying in the road, picked it up and put it in his basement.
Yasgur refused to rent out his farm for a 1970 revival of the event,
saying that he was going back to running a dairy farm. In April
2011, Guernsey's of New York were negotiating a private sale of the
sign for an undisclosed sum.

$20,000–$30,000

James Dean's ID bracelet

Sterling-silver ID bracelet belonging to James Byron Dean
(1931–55). The reverse of the plate is inscribed with the legend
'D.D.-1955'. The initials stand for 'Dilemma Dean', the enigmatic
nickname the star was given by friends. Dean died when his Porsche
550 Spyder collided with an oncoming car on US Route 466, San
Luis Obispo County, on 30 September 1955. He was 24. The bracelet
was offered for sale at auction by Guernsey's in January 2011 with an
estimate of $20,000–$30,000.

Dillinger's 'pistol'

Wooden facsimile pistol used by John Herbert
Dillinger (1903–34), America's first 'Public Enemy
No. 1', to break out from the Crown Point jail,
Indiana, on 3 March 1934. Sequestered at the county jail (that the
authorities boasted was 'escape-proof') to await trial for the murder
of an East Chicago police officer, Dillinger managed to smuggle the
dummy pistol into his cell with the help of his attorney. Using it to
trick the nearest guard into opening his cell, Dillinger took two men
hostage, rounded up all the prison officers, locked them in his cell
and fled with a parting taunt to his erstwhile custodians, 'See what
I locked all of you monkeys up with? Nothing but a little piece of
wood.' After a nationwide FBI manhunt led by special agent Melvin
Purvis, Dillinger was tracked down four months later to Chicago,
where, after a tip-off from a brothel madame, he was gunned down
by Federal agents outside the Biograph movie theatre on 22 July
1934. The 'pistol', with 'Colt 38' carved into it, was sold by Heritage
Auctions in Dallas for $19,120.

$19,120

Damien's tricycle

Tricycle ridden by British child actor Harvey Stephens as Damien Thorn in Richard Donner's 1976 film *The Omen*. In one of the most notorious scenes of the film, Damien, aka Son of Satan, born of a goat, crashes the machine into a chair on which his mother is standing, sending her plunging over the banisters to her death. Offered for sale by Bonhams in December 2010, with an estimate of £15,000.

The Ten Commandments

Two 23in x 12in 'tablets' carried by Charlton Heston as Moses in Cecil B. DeMille's 1956 film *The Ten Commandments*. The round-topped fibreglass panels, resembling reddish, speckled stone, and engraved with linguistically accurate Palaeo-Hebrew inscriptions, were offered for sale at auction by Guernsey's in New York in January 2010 with an estimate of $30,000–$40,000.

$30,000–$40,000

Earhart's goggles

Goggles worn by Amelia Mary Earhart (1897–1937) during her historic transatlantic flight in 1932, the first non-stop solo crossing ever made by a woman. On the morning of 20 May, Earhart and her single-engined Lockheed Vega 5b took off from Harbour Grace, Newfoundland, heading for Paris. After a flight lasting 14 hours and 56 minutes, during which she contended with strong northerly winds, icy conditions and mechanical problems, Earhart landed in a pasture at Culmore, north of Derry, Northern Ireland. When a farmhand asked, 'Have you flown far?' Earhart replied, 'From America.' During an attempt to make a circumnavigational flight of the globe in 1937 in a Purdue-funded Lockheed Model 10 Electra, Earhart disappeared over the central Pacific Ocean near Howland Island. Neither the aircraft nor her remains were ever found. The goggles were sold at auction by Profiles in History, California, in October 2009 for $141,600.

$141,600

Dettori's goggles

Racing goggles worn by Lanfranco 'Frankie' Dettori (1970–)
during his 'Magnificent Seven' race day at Ascot on 28 September
1996, when the Italian rode to victory in all seven races on the
card. The BBC halted its organised programming to broadcast the
last race live as bookmakers slashed the odds on Dettori's final
mount, Fujiyama Crest, from 12–1 to 2–1 favourite. He won the
race by a length. The historic 25,051–1 seven-timer reportedly lost
bookmakers £30 million. After the seventh race, BetFred's Fred
Done flashed a message on to the screens of all his betting
shops: 'Reward, dead or alive: good-looking Italian
kid, last seen in Ascot area.' The goggles were
offered for sale by Paul Fraser Collectibles in April
2011 for £15,000.

£15,000

THROUGH THE LOOKING-GLASS,

AND WHAT ALICE FOUND THERE.

Alice's own *Through the Looking-Glass*

1871 first edition of *Through the Looking-Glass, and What Alice Found There* by Lewis Carroll, once belonging to Alice Pleasance Liddell (1852–1934). On 4 July 1862, while travelling by rowing boat from Folly Bridge, Oxford, to Godstow on a picnic outing, ten-year-old Alice challenged family friend and Oxford mathematician Charles Lutwidge Dodgson (1832–98) to entertain her and her sisters with a story. As the Reverend Robinson Duckworth plied the oars, Dodgson regaled the girls with fantastic stories of a girl named Alice and her adventures after she fell into a rabbit-hole. The story, of which Alice begged a written copy, formed the basis for *Alice's Adventures in Wonderland*, published in 1865 under the pseudonym Lewis Carroll. *Through the Looking-Glass, and What Alice Found There* followed as a sequel in 1871. This copy of the book, signed 'Alice Pleasance Liddell' and including an acrostic poem at the back, spelling out her full name, was sold at auction by Profiles in History, California, in December 2009 for $115,000.

London Calling

Artwork from the 1979 album *London Calling* by The Clash. The cover features a photograph by Pennie Smith (who considered the shot too out of focus to be used) of bass guitarist Paul Simonon smashing his Fender Precision Bass against the stage at The Palladium in New York on 21 September 1979 during the 'Clash Take the Fifth' US tour. Designed by graphic designer Ray Lowry, the cover was intended as an ironic homage to the cover of Elvis's debut album. In 2002, Smith's photograph was named the best rock and roll photograph of all time by Q magazine, citing the fact that 'it captures the ultimate rock'n'roll moment – total loss of control'. The cover artwork was sold at auction by Bonhams in December 2009 for £72,000.

£72,000

The Pope's cross

Pectoral cross once belonging to Pope Paul VI (Giovanni Battista
Enrico Antonio Maria Montini, 1897–1978). The cross (pectoral
crosses being awarded to Catholics who reach the status of bishop
or higher) comprises 12 main diamonds weighing over 60cts
surrounded by hundreds of smaller diamonds and emeralds. It was
donated by Pope Paul VI to the United Nations in 1965, to be sold
and the money used for humanitarian purposes. The cross has since
passed through a number of hands, including those of U Thant of
the United Nations and daredevil Evel Knievel, before
being brought into the jewellery emporium of Alan
Perry, a Southern Baptist, who offered it for sale on
eBay for $850,000.

$850,000

$1,500

Jim Morrison's sunglasses

Aviator-style sunglasses with gold-coloured wire frame, plastic bridge and green glass lenses, once belonging to James Douglas 'Jim' Morrison (1943–71). One of 15 similar but slightly different pairs originally made for Morrison by Dennis Roberts of Optique Originals in Hollywood, the glasses were sold at auction by Guernsey's in September 2010 for $1,500.

Fischer-Spassky chess set

Original World Chess Championship chess set used by Robert
James 'Bobby' Fischer (1943–2008) and Boris Vasilievich Spassky
(1937–) in their legendary 'Match of the Century'. On 11 July 1972,
with a presidential crisis stirring in the USA and the Cold War at
a pivotal point, Spassky, the (refreshingly un-Soviet) Soviet World
Chess Champion, and Fischer, his American challenger, sat down*
opposite each other in Reykjavik's Laugardalshöll arena to contest
what was to be the most documented and notorious chess match
of all time. Over the next two months, Spassky, a chess-playing
machine who had returned the title to the Kremlin for years, and
Fischer, a 29-year-old goofy and egocentric loner from Brooklyn,
riveted the chess-playing and non-chess-playing world as they
vied not only for the ultimate prize in chess but for intellectual
hegemony of their respective political systems. Fischer's victory
(12^{1}/$_{2}$–8^{1}/$_{2}$) ended 24 years of Soviet domination of the world
championship and was viewed with elation by the Western world.
Presented to Guomundur Thorarinsson, the President of the
Icelandic Chess Federation, as a birthday present in 1972, this set

*Fischer insisted on being seated on an Eames Executive Chair, claiming that it helped
him concentrate. Spassky later requested the same type of chair, which was delivered
for him in time for Game 7.

is one of three that were used during the 52-day struggle. It was on this set that the notorious third 'Back Room Game'* was played. Signed by Fischer and, one has to feel, magnanimously, by Spassky, the set was sold at auction by Philip Weiss in April 2011 for $76,275.

*After a shaky start by the challenger, Fischer asked, in a typical act of gamesmanship (chess supremo Garry Kasparov later commented that Fischer had won the title away from the board as much as on it), that the third game be played away from the public and the media. Spassky manfully acceded to the request and the game was played in a back room of the venue. Fischer won this third game, a victory that proved to be the turning-point of the match.

Jaws' jaws

7ft x 11ft jaw of a Megalodon shark, the largest predator ever to have existed on earth. Growing to 50 feet long (equivalent to two city buses) and weighing 100 tons, the Megalodon (translated from the Greek as 'big tooth') lorded it over temperate, coastal waters from 25 to 1.5 million years ago, during the Cenozoic era. Exerting a biting force of over 18 tons, the Megalodon preyed on cetaceans, mainly sperm whales and bowhead whales, snacking occasionally on porpoises, dolphins and giant turtles. Contrary to the hunting strategies of existing shark species, this oceanic boss of bosses would focus on the tough skeletal portions (i.e. shoulders, flippers, ribcage and upper spine) of its prey, sinking its 182 7in teeth into the bones and thereby fatally damaging the internal organs. The dead or dying victims could then be ingested at leisure. This Megalodon jaw, the largest ever assembled, was put together over a 16-year period by jeweller and amateur scuba diver Vito Bertucci from fossils collected from the shores of South Carolina rivers. Bertucci was drowned in October 2004 in the Ogeechee River south of Savannah, Georgia, while diving for further remnants of the great fish. The jaw was offered for sale at auction on behalf of his brother by Heritage Auction Galleries in June 2011, with an estimate of $700,000.

$700,000

Lincoln's opera glasses

$700,000

Black and gold-framed opera glasses used by
Abraham Lincoln (1809–65) on the evening he was
assassinated by John Wilkes Booth. After attending a speech in
which Lincoln promoted voting rights for blacks, an enraged
Booth, a well-known actor and Confederate spy, formulated a plan
to murder Lincoln three days later while he attended a performance
of *Our American Cousin* at Ford's Theatre in Washington, DC. During
the intermission, Lincoln's bodyguard, John Parker, left the theatre
to join Lincoln's coachman for drinks in the Star Saloon next
door. Seizing the opportunity, Booth crept up from behind and at
about 10.13 p.m. fired point blank into the back of Lincoln's head,
mortally wounding the president. After being in a coma for nine
hours, Lincoln died at 7.22 a.m. on 15 April. Booth was executed
by Union soldiers on 26 April. Recovered from the president's box
by an army officer shortly after the fatal shot was fired, the glasses
were offered for sale at auction by Sotheby's, New York, in June 2011
with an estimate of $700,000.

Solidarity HQ sign

58in x 36in sign that hung from the 1989 Gdansk headquarters
of Solidarity, the non-Communist Polish trade union federation
founded by Lech Wałęsa and others in September 1980. Advocating
non-violence from its members, the movement resisted the
government's attempts to destroy it with the imposition of martial
law in 1981 and finally forced their Soviet leaders to the negotiating
table in 1989. The round-table talks led to semi-free elections,
through which Tadeusz Mazowiecki was installed as prime minister
at the head of a Solidarity-led coalition. Solidarity benefited
very considerably from the intercession and support of Polish-
born Karol Wojtyła (1920–2005), Pope John Paul II, whose 1987
encyclical *Solicitudo Rei Socialis* identified the concept of solidarity
with the poor and marginalised as a constitutive element of the
Gospel and human participation in the common good. Polish
workers closely associated themselves with the Church, frequently
displaying images of Pope John Paul or the Virgin Mary. The success
of Solidarity not only marked a break with the hardline stance of the
Communist Polish United Workers' Party and the wider Communist
regime, but also served to inspire the effective dismantling of the
Eastern Bloc and the eventual dissolution of Soviet rule.
Signed by nine world leaders of the period, the
sign was offered for sale by Signature Auctions in
September 2010 with an estimate of $40,000.

$40,000

Hemingway's elephant gun

1913 double-barrelled .577-calibre Nitro Express
rifle by Westley Richards, once belonging to
journalist, author, hunter and adventurer Ernest Miller
Hemingway (1899–1961). Weighing in at nearly 16lb, the rifle was
designed to stop the biggest beasts in Africa. As well as taking it
on safari, Hemingway also kept the gun aboard his fishing boat
Pilar during the Second World War, fancying that if the weapon was
substantial enough to take down elephants and rhinos, it stood
every chance of making a hole in the hulls of German U-boats,
which often infiltrated the waters off Cuba. Sadly, he never had the
chance to test this ballistic theory. Hemingway had an elemental
love for firearms (he was taught to shoot at the age of two and a
half, and was reportedly reasonably proficient with a pistol aged
four). Indeed, a 184-page book, Hemingway's Guns by Silvio Calabi
(2010), was recently devoted to his collection. Hemingway shot
himself with his favourite W. & C. Scott & Son pigeon gun at his
home in Ketchum, Idaho, on 2 July 1961. His Westley Richards
was sold by James D. Julia Auctioneers in Maine in March 2011 for
$339,250.

$339,250

$300,000+

Photograph of Billy the Kid

The single known authenticated photograph of William H. Bonney, 'Billy the Kid' (1859–81). The 2in x 3in tintype shows the outlaw in a gambling hall in Fort Sumner, New Mexico, in 1880, the year before he was finally gunned down at the house of his friend Pete Maxwell just outside the town by Sheriff Pat Garrett on 21 July 1881. The photograph was offered for sale at the Denver Merchandise Mart, Colorado, in June 2011, with an estimate of $300,000–$400,000.

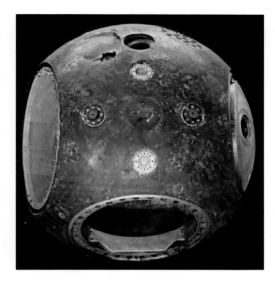

Ivan Ivanovich's space capsule

$2.9m

Vostok 3KA-2. Aluminium test space capsule despatched by
the Russians into space on 9 March 1961. Launched a month before
Yuri Gagarin's first manned mission in *Vostok 3KA-3*, *Vostok 3KA-2*
was 'piloted' by 'Ivan Ivanovich', the name given to a cosmonaut-
suited mannequin used to test the craft. Also containing a dog
named Zvezdochka, various reptiles and 80 mice and guinea pigs
(some of which were stuffed inside Ivanovich's body), the capsule
completed one full orbit of the earth, re-entered the atmosphere
and landed after 115 minutes in a valley near to the city of Izhevsk
in the Western Urals. Thirty Russian paratroopers recovered the
capsule, using a peasant's horse-drawn sleigh. Ejected on descent,
Ivan was found intact with his parachute close by. Zvezdochka
emerged from the capsule unharmed. The world's first spacecraft
was sold at auction by Sotheby's in April 2011 for $2.9 million.

Spock's ear

Prosthetic pointed ear worn by Leonard Nimoy as Captain Kirk's half-human, half-Vulcan sidekick Mr Spock in the 1979 film *Star Trek*. Offered for sale by Premiere Props in Los Angeles in April 2011, with an estimate of $700.

$700

Chitty Chitty Bang Bang

$1–$2m

Iconic 'flying' car used in Ken Hughes's 1968 film based on Ian Fleming's 1964 children's novel *Chitty Chitty Bang Bang: The Magical Car*. Designed by the film's production designer, Ken Adam, and cartoonist and sculptor Frederick Roland Emett, the car was built by Alan Mann Racing in Hertfordshire in 1967, fitted with a Ford 3000 V6 engine and automatic transmission and allocated its own genuine UK registration: GEN 11. Fleming took his inspiration for the car from a series of aero-engined racing cars built by Count Louis Zborowski in the early 1920s at Higham Park in Kent, christened 'Chitty Bang Bang'. Belonging to Pierre Picton (stand-in driver for Dick Van Dyke as Caractacus Potts in the film) since the early 1970s, the car was sold at auction by Profiles in History in Los Angeles in May 2011 with an estimate of $1–$2 million.

Untitled #96

Untitled #96, a 1981 self-portrait by Cindy Sherman (1954–). Sold at auction by Christie's in May 2011 for $3.89 million. The most expensive photograph in history.

$3.89m

$800,000–$1.2m

The Nonsuch Palace

1572 watercolour by Joris Hofnagel of the south frontage of the Nonsuch Palace, the only surviving representation of King Henry VIII's most grandiose of building projects. Designed to outshine the French King Francis I's Château de Chambord in the Loire Valley, the palace was begun on the site of Cuddington village in Surrey on 22 April 1538 (the village was laid waste to make way for its construction) and completed nine years and £24,000 later. It was called 'Nonsuch' due to the contention that no other king's residence could equal its magnificence. The vast symbol of Tudor power was pulled down in 1682 to pay off the gambling debts of Charles II's mistress, Barbara, Countess of Castlemaine, to whom he had gifted the palace. Hofnagel's painting was sold at auction by Christie's in December 2010 with an estimate of £800,000–£1.2 million.

John James Audubon's *Birds of America*

£7.3m

1827 first edition of *Birds of America* by French-American ornithologist, naturalist, hunter and painter John James Audubon (1785–1851). Comprising 435 life-sized, hand-coloured prints made from engravings of Audubon's watercolours (each taking the artist approximately 60 hours to complete), the 3ft x 2ft book from the collection of Lord Hesketh was sold at auction by Sotheby's in December 2010 for £7,321,250, making it the most expensive printed book in history.

The General Lee

Modified 1969 Dodge Charger driven by the Duke cousins Bo and
Luke in the Warner Bros 1979–85 television series *The Dukes
of Hazzard*. Offered for sale by Volocars.com in June
2011 with an estimate of $150,000.

$150,000

£5,200

The first snap of Burton and Taylor

1962 photograph of Richard Burton and Elizabeth Taylor together at Dame Gracie Fields's La Canzone Del Mare hotel on the island of Capri, shortly before their adulterous relationship was made public. They had begun their relationship during the making of Joseph L. Mankiewicz's 1963 film *Cleopatra* in Rome. News of Burton and Taylor's affair, days after this photograph was taken, caused an international media frenzy and widespread opprobrium. Notable in their condemnation were US Representative Iris Blitch, who introduced a bill in the US Congress to have both stars banned from entering the USA, and *L'Osservatore della Domenica*, the Vatican City's weekly, that accused Taylor of 'erotic vagrancy'. Despite the personal and professional fall-out of their romance – not to mention the toll on their psychological and physical health (in a 1973 *Parkinson* interview, Burton admitted to consuming three bottles of hard liquor a day at one point) – the couple's attachment famously and irresistibly endured. Burton wrote Taylor a love letter two days before he died from a brain haemorrhage on 5 August 1984. Taylor, who died from congestive heart failure on 23 March 2011, asked to be buried with it. The photograph was contained within a scrapbook belonging to Gracie Fields which was sold at auction by Gorringe's of Lewes, East Sussex, in May 2010 for £5,200.

£950

Dickens's inkwell

Brass inkwell once belonging to Charles Dickens (1812–70).
Used by the author at his home, Gad's Hill, at Higham in Kent,
in the writing of his last novel, *The Mystery of Edwin Drood*, which
remained unfinished before his death from a stroke on 9 June
1870. The inkwell was sold at auction by Dickins Auctioneers,
Buckinghamshire, for £950.

Hitler versus Lenin

1909 etching depicting Adolf Hitler and Vladimir Lenin playing chess. The picture, purportedly signed on the reverse by the two notorious ideologues, is said to be the work of Hitler's art teacher in Vienna, Emma Lowenstramm, at a time when Hitler was a jobbing artist in the city and Lenin was in exile from Russia. Although historians have cast doubt on whether such a contest ever took place, the unnamed vendor's father compiled a 300-page document, including the results of tests on the paper and the signatures, attesting to the image's authenticity. Richard Westwood-Brookes, of auctioneers Mullock's, said, 'The signatures in pencil are said to have an 80 per cent chance of being genuine.' Offered for sale by Mullock's in Shropshire in October 2010 with an estimate of £10,000–£15,000.

£10,000–£15,000

£430,000

Hunt's Hesketh

Formula 1 Hesketh racing car, chassis 308/2, driven to victory in the 1975 Dutch Grand Prix in Zandvoort by James Simon Wallis Hunt (1947–93). Hesketh Racing, founded in 1972, originally competed with little success with Hunt in Formula Three until the flamboyant Lord Hesketh announced that, as the costs were nearly the same, they 'might as well lose in Formula One as Three'. After two years of development at Hesketh's Easton Neston estate under the auspices of designer Harvey Postlethwaite, Hunt and 308/2 (complete with the Hesketh teddy bear logo) held off Nikki Lauda in the final lap at Zandvoort to take the chequered flag for his first and Hesketh's only Grand Prix win. Hunt went on to win the World Championship in 1976 with McLaren. He died of a heart attack in 1993. Still in the ownership of Lord Hesketh, this, the last privately entered car to win a Grand Prix without commercial sponsorship, was offered for sale at Silverstone Auctions in July 2011 with an estimate of £430,000.

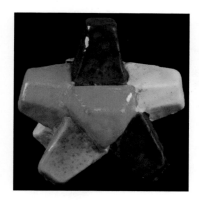

Everlasting Gobstopper

Everlasting Gobstopper used in Mel Stuart's 1971 musical *Willy Wonka and the Chocolate Factory*. The Everlasting Gobstopper first appeared in Roald Dahl's 1964 children's book *Charlie and the Chocolate Factory*. They were designed by the factory's proprietor, Willy Wonka, for children with 'very little pocket-money'. Offered for sale at auction by Profiles in History in May 2011 with an estimate of $15,000–$20,000.

$15,000–$20,000

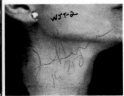

Lennon's last autograph

$532,000

Double Fantasy LP cover signed by John Winston
Ono Lennon (1940–80) for his killer, Mark David
Chapman (1955–), five hours before Chapman shot him.
On the morning of 8 December 1980, Chapman, a 25-year-old
former YMCA summer camp counsellor and depressive, left his
room at the Sheraton Hotel in New York and made for the Dakota
Building on Central Park West and 72nd Street, the apartment
block in which Lennon and Yoko Ono had become resident. During
the day, which he spent loitering outside the entrance, Chapman
encountered five-year-old Sean Lennon with his nanny; he shook
Sean's hand and called him a 'beautiful boy'. At around 5.00 p.m.,
Lennon and Ono left the Dakota for a recording session at Record
Plant Studios. As they walked towards their limousine at the kerb,
Chapman shook hands with Lennon and held out a copy of *Double
Fantasy*, which Lennon signed. It wasn't until five hours later that
the Lennons' limousine returned to the Dakota, where Chapman
was still patiently waiting. At the kerb, Lennon and Ono got out,
passed Chapman and walked towards the archway entrance of
the building's courtyard. From the street behind them, reportedly
dropping into a 'combat stance' and calling softly 'Mr Lennon',
Chapman fired five hollow-point bullets from a .38 Special revolver,
four of them hitting Lennon in the back and left shoulder. Rushed
from the scene by responding police officers to St Luke's-Roosevelt

Hospital Center, Lennon was pronounced dead at 11.15 p.m. Chapman, meanwhile, remained where he was and was arrested without protest, still holding the gun and a copy of J. D. Salinger's 1951 novel *The Catcher in the Rye*, which he had inscribed with the words: 'This is my statement. (signed) Holden Caulfield.' In a statement to police three hours later, Chapman said, 'I'm sure the large part of me is Holden Caulfield, who is the main person in the book. The small part of me must be the Devil.' Chapman is currently imprisoned at the Attica Correctional Facility in Attica, New York. He has been denied parole six times. Signed 'John Lennon 1980', the album cover was sold at auction by Moments in Time in December 2010 for $532,000.

JFK's last autograph

Front page of the *Dallas Morning News* morning edition of 22 November 1963, bearing what is believed to be the last signature of President John Fitzgerald 'Jack' Kennedy (1917–63). Early that morning, while Kennedy was on his way to give a breakfast speech before the Fort Worth, Texas, Chamber of Commerce, a hotel housekeeper by the name of Jan White approached the president and his Secret Service detail in the hallway of the Texas Hotel and asked him to sign her copy of the newspaper. The inscription reads 'To Jan White. John Kennedy'. Approximately four hours later, at 12.30 p.m. Central Standard Time, Kennedy was assassinated in Dealey Plaza. Offered for sale by Heritage Auctions in November 2009, the newspaper was bought by Joseph Maddalena, the president of Profiles in History, the California auction house, for $39,000.

Tommy Cooper's fez

Burgundy wool fez with a black silk tassel, once belonging to Thomas Frederick 'Tommy' Cooper (1921–84). The fez was sold at auction by Christie's in November 2010 for £4,750.

£4,750

€45,000

Checkpoint Bravo

Main autobahn border crossing point between West Berlin and the German Democratic Republic during the Cold War. Including a derelict bridge and a crumbling café covered in graffiti, the site was sold at auction in September 2010 for €45,000.

R. D. 2
Windsor, Vt.
July 19, 1957

Dear Mr. Herbert,

I'll try to tell you what my attitude is to the stage and screen rights of The Catcher in the Rye. I've sung this tune quite a few times, so if my heart doesn't seem to be in it, try to be tolerant....Firstly, it is possible that one day the rights will be sold. Since there's an ever-looming possibility that I won't die rich, I toy very seriously with the idea of leaving the unsold rights to my wife and daughter as a kind of insurance policy. It pleasures me no end, though, I might quickly add, to know that I won't have to see the results of the transaction. I keep saying this and nobody seems to agree, but The Catcher in the Rye is a very novelistic novel. There are readymade "scenes" - only a fool would deny that - but, for me, the weight of the book is in the narrator's voice, the non-stop peculiarities of it, his personal, extremely discriminating attitude to his reader-listener, his asides about gasoline rainbows in street puddles, his philosophy or way of looking at cowhide suitcases and empty toothpaste cartons - in a word, his thoughts. He can't legitimately be separated from his own first-person technique. True, if the separation is forcibly made, there is enough material left over for something called an Exciting (or maybe just Interesting) Evening in the Theater. But I find that idea if not odious, at least odious enough to keep me from selling the rights. There are many of his thoughts, of course, that could be labored into dialogue - or into some sort of stream-of-consciousness loud-speaker device - but labored is exactly the right word. What he thinks and does so

??????

Salinger's 'no'

Ever since The Catcher in the Rye was published in 1951, a steady stream of producers, directors, screenwriters and actors has attempted unsuccessfully to secure the film rights to J. D. Salinger's seminal novel. This letter of 19 July 1957 from the author to a Mr Herbert, sold at auction by Moments in Time for an undisclosed sum, outlines with (we think) arresting eloquence, insight and grace the reluctance of his creator to allow Holden Caulfield to appear on screen.

naturally in his solitude in the novel, on the stage could at best
only be pseudo-simulated, if there is such a word (and I hope not).

Not to mention, God help us all, the immeasurably risky business
of using actors. Have you ever seen a child actress sitting crosslegged
on a bed and looking right? I'm sure not. And Holden Caulfield
himself, in my undoubtedly super-biassed opinion, is essentially
unactable. A Sensitive, Intelligent, Talented Young Actor in
a Reversible Coat wouldn't be nearly enough. It would take
someone with X to bring it off, and no very young man even if he
has X quite knows what to do with it. And, I might add, I don't
think any director can tell him.
            I'll stop there. I'm afraid I can only tell you,
to end with, that I feel very firm about all this, if you haven't
already guessed.

            Thank you, though, for your friendly and highly
readable letter. My mail from producers has mostly been hell.

                              Sincerely,

                              J. D. Salinger

The Seventh Seal chess set

Plaster and wooden chess pieces used in Ingmar Bergman's 1957 film *The Seventh Seal*, in which the medieval knight Antonius Block (played by Max von Sydow) famously challenges the personification of Death (Bengt Ekerot) to a game of chess in order to delay his own demise. Death (playing black) wins. The pieces were sold at auction by Bukowski's in Stockholm in September 2009 for 1 million Swedish crowns (£90,250).

£90,250

Hawaii 5-0 badge

$1,000–$1,500

'Book 'em, Danno. Murder One.' Original police badge, reading 'State of Hawaii Investigator Five-O Unit', used on the long-running CBS series based around a fictional state police unit run by Jack Lord's Detective Steve McGarrett and featuring Morton Stevens's infectious theme music. Owned by the estate of Jack Lord, the badge was offered for sale at auction by Bonhams in June 2011 with an estimate of $1,000–$1,500.

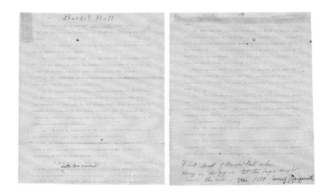

The rules of basketball

Two-page typed document bearing the original 13 rules of basketball, as laid out in December 1891 by the game's inventor, James A. Naismith (1861–1939). Struggling as a teacher at the YMCA International Training School in Springfield, Massachusetts, with a recalcitrant class who were confined indoors throughout the harsh New England winter, Naismith was challenged by the Head of Physical Education, Dr Luther Gulick, to create, in 14 days, a new game that would keep his track athletes in shape and be 'fair for all players and not too rough'. Naismith's solution was informed by three insights: firstly, that there were inherent hazards in a small, fast ball, as used in hockey or baseball; secondly, that most physical contact occurred while running with, dribbling or hitting a ball; and thirdly, that physical contact could further be reduced by making the 'goals' unguardable. His resulting game, originally played using a pair of suspended peach baskets, is now played by more than 300 million people worldwide. This document, the birth certificate of basketball, was sold at auction by Sotheby's in December 2010 for $4.4 million.

$4.4m

3 Fair Catch is a Catch ... entitles a free Kick

4 Charging is fair in case of a place kick (with the exception of a kick off) as soon as the player offers to kick, but he may always draw back unless he has actually touched the Ball with his foot

5 No pushing with the Hands or Hacking or tripping is fair under any circumstances whatsoever

6 Knocking or pushing on the ball is altogether disallowed — the side breaking this Rule forfeits a free kick to the opposite side

7 No player may be held or pulled over

8 It is not lawful to take the Ball off the Ground (except in touch) for any purpose whatever

9 If the Ball be ... it may be stopped by the hand but not pushed or hit ... it may not be stopped ...

10 No Goal may be kicked from touch nor by a free kick from a Catch

11 A Ball in touch is dead. consequently, the side that touches it down, must bring it to the edge of touch, & throw it straight out at least six yards from touch

£1.2m

The rules of football

Handwritten 1858 pamphlet outlining the rules of club football for the first time. Compiled by the ex-public school boys who founded the Sheffield Football Association – today's Sheffield United – in 1857 (making it the world's oldest football club), the document introduces rules that still exist, such as the indirect free kick, the corner kick and the use of a crossbar. Another rule states, somewhat liberally: 'Pushing with the hands is allowed but no hacking or tripping is fair under any circumstances whatsoever.' Although the sport had been previously codified in 1848 at Trinity College, Cambridge, by public school representatives from Eton, Harrow, Rugby, Winchester and Shrewsbury, the Sheffield Rules were the first 'democratic' guidelines for how the beautiful game should be played. Currently owned by Sheffield FC, the 'ultimate prize in football memorabilia' was offered for sale by Sotheby's in July 2011 with an estimate (as part of a larger archive) of £1.2 million.

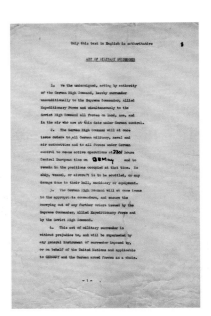

'The German Instrument of Surrender'

'The German Instrument of Surrender', being the unconditional surrender of the German Third Reich, signed at 0241 hours, 7 May 1945, in the war room at Supreme Headquarters, Allied Expeditionary Force, located in the Professional and Technical School at Reims, northern France, signalling the end of the Second World War in Europe. Signatories to the document were as follows: the German Colonel General Alfred Jodl, delegated by the now President Doenitz on behalf of the German High Command; US Lieutenant General Walter Bedell Smith, representing General Eisenhower (who refused to meet the Germans until the surrender had been signed); Soviet Major General Ivan Sousloparov, fulfilling the Big Three agreement that a Soviet representative would take

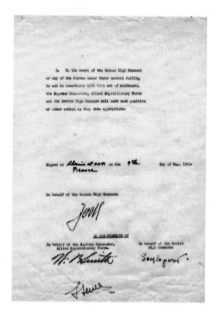

part in any ceremony of total surrender; and Major General François Sevez, signing as a witness for France. It is interesting to note that the signature of the French representative was made in the lower margin of the document, reportedly because the Germans did not consider the French to be equal to the Americans, British and Russians and therefore insisted that their signature should not appear on the main document. Following the event, Eisenhower gave this copy, one of four originals signed at the time, to his adjutant, from whose estate the document was obtained. The document was offered for sale by Moments in Time in June 2011 for $2.5 million.

$2.5m

Yale's secret skull and bones

1872 human skull (with hinged flap) and bones once used as a
ballot box at meetings of Yale University's elite secret society,
Skull and Bones. Founded in 1832, the society has had a defining
influence over the American establishment – its members, known
as 'Bonesmen', have reportedly included President William Howard
Taft, President George H. W. Bush, his son, President George W.
Bush, Senator John Kerry, Stephen A. Schwarzman, Founder of
Blackstone, Austan Goolsbee, Chairman of President Obama's
Council of Economic Advisers, and Harold Stanley, co-founder
of Morgan Stanley. The society is believed to be such a formative
influence in the US corridors of power that the 2006 spy film *The
Good Shepherd* suggested that a man could become CIA director only
if he belonged to Skull and Bones – a claim officially rejected by the
CIA. Every year Skull and Bones selects 15 final-year Yale students
to join its ranks with a tap on the shoulder and the question: 'Skull
and Bones, accept or reject?' The society's many rituals reportedly
include nude wrestling and confessing one's sexual secrets while
lying in a coffin. This macabre artefact of the rather dubious yet
fascinating organisation was offered for sale at auction
by Christie's in January 2010 with an estimate of
$10,000–$20,000.

$10,000–$20,000

The Vieuxtemps Guarneri

$18m

1741 violin by Bartolomeo Giuseppe Antonio Guarneri
(1698–1744). It is commonly assumed (not least by
the authors) that, in the field of instrument-making, the creations
of Antonio Stradivari (1644–1737) are without equal. But for
many connoisseurs and concert performers the work of Guarneri
represents the true pinnacle of the art. Indeed, the relative merits
of the two Cremona craftsmen's creations are a clichéd topic
among violin aficionados. The issue of rarity, of course, can skew
the argument (Stradivari lived to 93, and about 640 of his violins
survive; Guarneri, by contrast, died in 1744 at 46, and only about
140 of his violins survive) but still it seems that Guarneri has the
lead over his older rival. Geoffrey Fushi, of specialist auctioneers
Bein & Fushi of Chicago, holds that the consensus is that 'a
Guarneri is like a rich chocolate, while a Strad is like strawberry or
vanilla ice cream. The Guarneri is often deeper, darker in sound.'
This particular Guarneri piece, named after Henri Vieuxtemps, a
19th-century musician who composed solo pieces for violin which
he performed using the instrument, is dubbed the 'Mona Lisa of
Violins' for its richness and power. Belonging to a retired British
financier and music philanthropist, Ian Stoutzker, the violin was
sold at auction by Bein & Fushi in July 2010 for $18 million, the
most expensive musical instrument in history.

'The Times They Are a-Changin''

Sheet of unruled three-hole notebook paper bearing the original, handwritten lyrics of the 1964 song 'The Times They Are a-Changin'' by Bob Dylan (born Robert Allen Zimmerman, 1941). As a sign that perhaps the 'times had changed' again, it is interesting to note that, in 1994, Dylan licensed his famous anthem of protest to be used in an advertisement for the auditing and accountancy firm Coopers & Lybrand and that, in 1996, a version of the song by Pete Seeger was used in an advertisement for the Bank of Montreal. The document was sold at auction by Sotheby's for $422,500 to collector and hedge-fund trader Adam Sender.

Herrmann's *Psycho*

£30,000–
£40,000

Original musical score by Bernard Herrmann
(1911–75) written for Alfred Hitchcock's 1960 film
Psycho. The music includes the 'shrieking violins' that accompany
the knife-in-the-shower scene. After the final 'silent' cut of the
film was first screened at Paramount in December 1959, neither
the studio nor Hitchcock himself was impressed. Hitchcock then
showed the film to Herrmann, who told the director to go home
for Christmas while he worked on the score. 'Well,' Hitchcock
reportedly replied, 'do what you like, but only one thing I ask of
you; please write nothing for the murder in the shower. That must
be without music.' Herrmann ignored him and composed what
has been described as the 'most famous cue in the history of film
music'. The score was offered for sale, on behalf of Herrmann's
widow, by Bonhams in March 2010 with an estimate of £30,000–
£40,000.

Facemash.com

Website created by Mark Elliot Zuckerberg (1984–) in October 2003 while attending Harvard University as a sophomore. The premise of Zuckerberg's invention was to juxtapose the university's private dormitory ID images (obtained by hacking into the protected areas of Harvard's computer network) and ask the audience to judge which of the students displayed was 'hotter'. The site attracted 450 visitors and 22,000 photo-views in its first four hours online, but was shut down a few days later by the Harvard administration. Zuckerberg was charged with breach of security, violating copyrights and violating individual privacy. Ultimately, however, the charges were dropped. The following semester, in January 2004, Zuckerberg began writing code for a new website and, on 4 February 2004, his social networking site, thefacebook.com, was launched. Seven years later, Facebook.com has over 500 million users (each having an average of 130 registered 'friends') and, following an investment by Goldman Sachs in January 2011, is valued at $50 billion. The anticipated flotation of the business could swell Zuckerberg's personal fortune to an estimated $13 billion. Zuckerberg's first online effort, on the other hand, was offered for sale in November 2010 for $35,000.

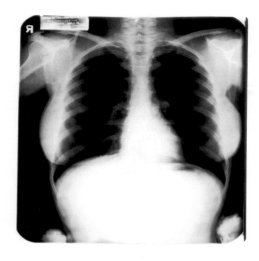

Marilyn Monroe's chest X-ray

X-ray image of the chest of Marilyn Monroe (1926–62), taken in November 1954 at the Cedars of Lebanon Hospital in Florida. A young doctor working at the hospital's medical school later obtained the X-ray and used it to hold the attention of his students. Belonging to the doctor's daughter, the X-ray was sold by Julien's Auctions in June 2010 for $45,000, 15 times its original estimate.

$45,000

13 Stars and Stripes

Original 13-star and 13-stripe US flag representing the 13 colonies (Delaware, Pennsylvania, New Jersey, Georgia, Connecticut, Massachusetts Bay, Maryland, South Carolina, New Hampshire, Virginia, New York, North Carolina, and Rhode Island and Providence) that rebelled against Britain in the American Revolution (1775–83). The Grand Union Flag (consisting of 13 red and white stripes with the British Union flag of the time in the canton) that was used by George Washington in the war has often been described as the United States' 'first national flag', but it has never had any official status. It did, however, inspire the design of the first official 'Stars and Stripes', which was enshrined in law on 14 June 1777 with the Marine Committee of the Second Continental Congress's Flag Resolution, which stated: 'Resolved, That the flag of the United States be thirteen stripes, alternate red and white; that the union be thirteen stars, white in a blue field, representing a new Constellation.' Stapled with a typewritten card reading, 'This 13 star flag is believed to have floated over Washington's headquarters at Newburgh,' the flag was sold at auction by Cowan's of Cincinnati in December 2010 for $10,575.

$10,575

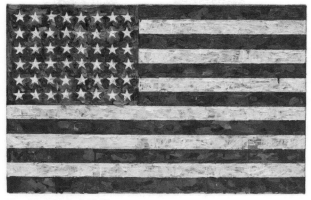

© Jasper Johns/VAGA, New York/DACS 2011

Johns's *Flag*

Flag, 1954–5, by Jasper Johns (1930–). Painted by Johns in his mid-twenties after having a dream of the American flag, the work was rendered with a difficult and seldom-used technique dating back to ancient Egypt: mixing paint pigment with hot wax and applying it in careful brushstrokes to the canvas. Part of the collection of Michael Crichton, *Flag* was sold at auction by Christie's in New York in May 2010 for $28,642,500.

$28.6m

Ayuba Suleiman Diallo

This 1733 oil painting of Ayuba Suleiman Diallo
(c. 1701–73) by William Hoare (c. 1707–92) is the first ever British
portrait of a freed slave. It depicts Diallo, a devout Muslim, with
his Qur'an (which he had written out from memory himself in
London), and was apparently made at the request of his English
friends despite his religious misgivings over being portrayed. Born
around 1701 into a wealthy and scholarly family of Muslim clerics
in Senegambia, West Africa, Diallo was highly educated and spoke
several languages. In 1730, however, he became a victim of the
ever-growing slave exploitation of the region, being captured near
the Gambia River by invading Mandingoes and sold to factors of the
Royal African Company. Despite protesting his exalted status, he
and his interpreter, Loumein Yoas, were shipped across the Atlantic
to the New World as slaves. Diallo was later rescued from a tobacco
plantation in Maryland by Thomas Bluett, an English lawyer and
missionary, and brought to England, where, 100 years before
the British abolition of slavery, he became a celebrity, meeting
George II and the intellectuals of the 1730s, and translating Arabic
documents and inscriptions for Sir Hans Sloane, whose collections
would become the nucleus of the British Museum. Slavery was
finally abolished throughout the British Empire by an Act of
Parliament given Royal Assent on 28 August 1833. The
painting was sold at auction by Christie's in January
2011 to the Qatar Museums Authority for £530,000.

£530,000

Ham the space chimp

Brass neck-tag once worn by Ham the chimpanzee, the first ever hominid launched into space. In the build-up to sending the first manned craft into orbit, the Holloman Aerospace Medical Center in New Mexico selected 40 chimpanzees as candidates for space flight. Of all the contenders put through training, one individual chimp stood out, an animal known only as 'Number 65'. (Mindful of the criticism the Russians received over the death of Laika the space dog on a trial mission four years earlier, the chimps were ascribed only numbers for fear of the publicity backlash of a named and therefore humanised animal perishing in space.) On 31 January 1961, aboard *Mercury-Redstone* 2, 'Number 65' flew 157 miles into space and reached a maximum velocity of 5,857 mph on his suborbital flight. Performing his tasks admirably, pushing levers no fewer than 50 times during the flight, hero Ham was finally given his name (an acronym of the lab that trained him) on his return to earth. After returning to the chimp colony at Holloman Air Force Base, Ham was trained for another planned flight but in the end never flew again. He passed his retirement in the National Zoo in Washington, DC, then at North Carolina Zoo, and died in 1983. Ham's neckwear was offered for sale at auction by Bonhams in May 2011 with an estimate of $2,000–$4,000.

$2,000–$4,000

The Murchison meteorite

$42,500

While the development of life over the past millions
of years is generally agreed by biological scientists to
have been explained through evolution by natural selection,
the beginning of life itself has proved a much thornier problem.
One possible theory that has gained some support over recent
years was precipitated (quite literally) at around 10.58 a.m. on
28 September 1969 by the arrival near Murchison, Victoria, in
Australia, of a particularly unusual piece of planetary debris after
its incoming bright fireball was observed by local villagers. The
100kg meteorite that had scattered itself over an area of 13 square
kilometres was found under examination to contain a mass of
organic compounds not present on earth, giving rise to the notion
that the earliest biochemicals necessary to life were not 'home-
grown' but imported by meteorite, lending powerful evidence to the
presence of extraterrestrial life. A slice of this much-studied alien
matter was offered for sale by Heritage Auctions in June 2011 with
an estimate of $42,500.

Camp X poison gas pen

Poison gas pen of the type issued to agents of the Special Operations Executive trained at the top-secret Camp X during the Second World War. Established on the north-western shore of Lake Ontario on 8 December 1941 by the chief of British Security Coordination, Sir William Stephenson, Camp X was designed for the purpose of training Allied agents intended to be dropped behind enemy lines as saboteurs and spies at a time when the Neutrality Act forbade US involvement in the war. More than 500 pupils (including the three Czech agents who went on to assassinate SS General Reinhard Heydrich in Prague in 1942) were schooled at Camp X in a wide variety of special techniques, including silent killing, sabotage, partisan support and recruitment methods for resistance movements, demolition, map reading, use of various weapons and Morse code. The camp's celebrated alumni included Ian Fleming. The poison gas pen formed part of a collection of Bond-style gadgets recovered when the camp closed in 1969 (including a dart-shooting camera, a dagger lipstick and exploding monkey dung) that were offered for sale on Barnstormers.com in May 2010 for $1 million.

?????

$117,000

The first lottery

Letter dated 31 August 1567 from Queen Elizabeth I (1533–1603)
to Sir John Spencer instructing him on the administration of
the country's first national lottery. The lottery involved 400,000
'tickets', each costing 10 shillings, with prizes (including a jackpot
of £5,000, a vast amount at that time) to be paid in a combination
of gold and merchandise, including tapestries, linens and fine
fabrics. It is not clear how or by whom the lottery was drawn, but
it reportedly took three years to hear whether you were among
the lucky winners. The monies raised, the letter states, shall be
'employed to good and publique acts and beneficially for o[u]r
Realme and o[u]r Subjects'. The Camelot of his time, Spencer
was promised 50 shillings for every £500 returned to London.
Queen Elizabeth's lottery died out, but other similar fund-raising
draws were held between 1750 and 1826. Signed with a flourishing
'Elizabeth R', the letter was sold in May 2010 for $117,000.

£102,700

112   Fath's bike

URS sidecar motorcycle on which Helmut Fath (1929–93) rode to
historic victory in the 1968 sidecar World Championship, a triumph
that crowned one of the most romantic stories in motorsport. In
1961, while heading for his second consecutive World Championship
with BMW, Fath crashed heavily at the Nürburgring in an accident
that killed his passenger, Alfred Wohlgemuth, and consigned Fath
to a year in hospital. Two years later, despite providing a superlative
(perhaps too superlative) tuning and preparation service for BMW
Rennsport engines at their Munich factory while he was physically
unfit to compete, Fath was rejected by the German giant when
he sought works support for his return to racing. The ex-world
champion remained undeterred. In a move inconceivable today,
Fath decided to go it alone. On a shoestring budget, in his forest
workshop outside the village of Ursenbach (from which the team
took its name), Fath began developing his own machine. With the
help of Dr Peter Kuhn of Heidelberg University and fellow racer/
engineer Horst Owesle, several steadily improving prototype
engines were created, each given their own name rather than
number (including 'Emil', 'Friedrich' and 'Heinrich') until finally
the 84–88bhp 'Gustav' was deemed race-perfect. It was therefore on
a motorcycle sidecar of his own design and engineering that Fath,
together with his passenger, Wolfgang Kalauch, overcame his old
employers to beat the BMW-mounted Johann Attenberger in 1968
and take the sidecar World Championship for a second time. Fath's
bike was sold at auction by Bonhams in October 2010 for £102,700.

HAL

£17,500

Front panel of the sentient on-board Heuristically
Programmed Algorithmic 9000 computer ('HAL')
on the Discovery One spacecraft in Arthur C. Clarke and Stanley
Kubrick's 1968 Warner Bros film *2001: A Space Odyssey*. Although
it is often conjectured that the name 'HAL' was based on a one-
letter alphabetical shift from the name of computer giant IBM ('H'
alphabetically precedes 'I', 'A' precedes 'B' and 'L' precedes 'M'),
this was denied by both Clarke and Kubrick. 'HAL' was sold at
auction by Christie's in November 2010 for £17,500.

Captain Scott's Union Jack

£73,250

Silk Union Jack taken on the 1912 British National
Antarctic Expedition to reach the South Pole, led
by Captain Robert Falcon Scott (1868–1912). Scott,
together with his chosen team of Edward Wilson, Henry Bowers,
Lawrence Oates and Edgar Evans, reached the Pole on 17 January
1912, only to find that his Norwegian rival, Roald Amundsen
(1872–1928) had beaten them to it, by some five weeks. On an icy
plateau, at the point where geographical coordinates are given as
simply 90°S, they found the Norwegian flag planted in triumph.
Scott's deflated party began their 850-mile trek back to base camp
on 19 January, a journey from which none of them would return. On
12 November 1912, Charles Seymour Wright, part of an eight-man
search party led by Royal Navy surgeon Edward Leicester Atkinson,
spotted the tent containing the bodies of Scott, Wilson and Bowers
(Evans and Oates having been lost prior to the expedition pitching
its final camp). The positions of the bodies suggested that Scott
had been the last of the three to die. As well as the flag and a
number of letters from Scott to Wilson's mother, Bowers's mother,
a string of notables (including his former commander Sir George
Egerton) and his own mother and wife, the search party recovered
Scott's diary. In it was included his 'Message to the Public', which
concluded with the words: 'We took risks, we knew we took them;
things have come out against us, and therefore we have no cause
for complaint, but bow to the will of Providence, determined still

to do our best to the last... Had we lived, I should have had a tale to tell of the hardihood, endurance, and courage of my companions which would have stirred the heart of every Englishman. These rough notes and our dead bodies must tell the tale, but surely, surely, a great rich country like ours will see that those who are dependent on us are properly provided for.' Scott gave up his diary on 23 March, save for one final entry on 29 March: 'For God's sake look after our people.' The bodies of the explorers were left where they were found. A high cairn of snow was erected over it, topped by a roughly fashioned cross. In January 1913, before *Terra Nova* (the ship in which Scott had embarked on the expedition) left for home, a large wooden cross was made by the ship's carpenters and erected as a permanent memorial on Observation Hill, overlooking Hut Point. The cross was inscribed with the names of the lost party and a line from Tennyson's poem *Ulysses*: 'To strive, to seek, to find, and not to yield'. Scott's Union Jack was sold at auction by Christie's in September 2010 for £73,250.

Fossett's car

$4m

Absolute land-speed-record car developed by the late
Steve Fossett's Reno, Nevada-based team during 2006–7. Fossett
bought the unfulfilled project in July 2006 from five-times world
land-speed-record holder Craig Breedlove. His initial target was
to achieve a record speed of 800 mph, with eventual development
planned for speeds of more than 900 mph. In September 2007, the
'Target 800 mph' team was nearing testing phase at Bonneville,
Utah, when Fossett was killed in his light aircraft. Dubbed 'Spirit
of America – Sonic Arrow', the car is constructed from a steel tube
frame with stressed aluminium skin and is powered by a General
Electric J-79 turbojet, as used in the USAF Phantom II fighter-
bomber. The engine generates over 18,400lb of supersonic thrust
with afterburner and water injection, and has a higher thrust-to-
weight ratio than any modern jet fighter. Mothballed for three
years, the car, together with all the equipment, designs and data of
the record-breaking project, was offered for sale in October 2010
for around $4 million, giving any buyer the opportunity to become,
however briefly, the fastest human being on earth.

Get in touch

If you'd like to contact us with any ideas for items that might be good to include in a future edition of 'desirable things', then we'd be delighted to hear from you. Please email us at:

Jolyon@2oltd.com
Marcus@2oltd.com

With many thanks,

Jolyon and Marcus

Acknowledgements

The authors would very much like to thank the following for their help in the creation of this book:

Momentsintime.com, International Autograph Auctions, Charles Miller, Anna Quattrini, Julien's Auctions, Sotheby's, Christie's, Bonhams, Lyon and Turnbull, Keys Auctioneers, Guernsey's, Paul Fraser Collectibles, Freeman's, RM Auctions, Mullock's, Cameo Auctioneers, Alexander Auctions, Lawrences of Crewkerne, Heritage Auctions, Profiles in History, Philip Weiss, Signature Auctions, James D. Julia Auctioneers, Premiere Props, Gorringe's of Lewes, Bein & Fushi, Cowan's of Cincinnati, Barnstormers.com, Silverstone Auctions, Potter and Potter Auctions, Volocars.com, James Fenwick, Martin Hattrell, Bill Husselby, Jill Husselby, Olivia Husselby, Andrew Franklin and Paul Forty.

Image credits

p. 14	Wall Street and Broad Street, original post-top style intersection street sign / The Bridgeman Art Library
p.35	First edition of the sheet music for 'The Star Spangled Banner' / The Bridgeman Art Library
p.53	Costume for Darth Vader from *Star Wars Episode V: The Empire Strikes Back*, 1980 / The Bridgeman Art Library
p.89	Burgundy wool fez with black silk tassel, signed inside by Tommy Cooper / The Bridgeman Art Library
p.106	Portrait of Ayuba Suleiman Diallo, 1733 (oil on canvas) by William Hoare of Bath (1707–92) / The Bridgeman Art Library
p.113	Hal 9000 computer faceplate from *2001: A Space Odyssey*, 1968 (20th Century) / The Bridgeman Art Library
p.114	Union Jack taken by Captain Scott on the British National Antarctic Expedition, 1901–03 / The Bridgeman Art Library